Hawai'i
on my mind

ANN CECIL

> " *It is a Sunday land. The land of indolence and dreams, where the air is drowsy and things tend to repose and peace, and to emancipation from the labor, and turmoil, and weariness, and anxiety of life.* "

Mark Twain

The
Globe
Pequot
Press

Guilford, Connecticut

" Never, even after all the times I have seen it, does this place fail to humble me, to make me marvel that the earth, the sky, and the sea can meet in such grandness. Silence, I believe, the silence of prayer, is the only manner in which a visitor can show his respect for such a gift."

O. A. Bushnell

Gentle waves caress the shore at tranquil Hamoa Beach near Hana, Maui.   LAURENCE PARENT

Lush tree ferns and giant bamboo lend a primeval beauty to 'Akaka Falls State Park, north of Hilo on the Big Island.   LARRY ULRICH

Tumbling falls feed the clear, inviting Pools of Ohe'o on the east end of Maui.   WILLIAM NEILL / LARRY ULRICH STOCK

Stately palms overlook the volcanic shoreline and turquoise waters of Pailoa Bay in remote Wai'anapanapa State Park, Maui. LAURENCE PARENT

" No alien land in all the world has any deep strong charm for me but that one, no other land could so longingly and so beseechingly haunt me, sleeping and waking, through half a lifetime, as that one has done.... For me its balmy airs are always blowing, its summer seas flashing in the sun; the pulsing of its surfbeat is in my ear; I can see its garlanded crags, its leaping cascades, its plumy palms drowsing by the shore...."

Mark Twain

The sea whittles the coastline along the rugged and isolated north shore of Moloka'i. JAMES RANDKLEV

From its throne of glossy green foliage, an elegant calla lily trumpets its presence. BRUCE JACKSON / GNASS PHOTO IMAGES

66 The Hawaiian rain forest gives off a wilderness sense that everything is in precisely the right place and the right condition of existence, everything connected with everything else, exactly as it should be. 99

Gavan Daws

Heliconia, often called "lobster claw," lends an exotic touch to tropical flower arrangements. BUDDY MAYS / TRAVEL STOCK

A tree fern shelters waxy, lipstick-red anthuriums in a Big Island garden.   BRUCE JACKSON / GNASS PHOTO IMAGES

Now a museum in Lahaina Harbor, the *Carthaginian* evokes images of bygone whaling days.   STEVE MULLIGAN

Sailors who have roamed the world still swear this…is the most haunting and beautiful place in all the Seven Seas.

Kiana Davenport

This salty old "sea captain" welcomes guests to the Pioneer Inn, on the Lahaina waterfront.   GREG VAUGHN

A humpback rewards patient whale watchers with an acrobatic full breach.   PHILLIP COLLA / INNERSPACE VISIONS
Photograph taken under provisions of NMFS Research Permit 633.

A fairy tern strikes a pose on Tern Island, one of the uninhabited
northwestern islands of the Hawaiian chain.   GREG VAUGHN

13

Kilauea Lighthouse, built in 1913, stands guard over a national wildlife refuge for boobies, shearwaters, and other sea birds on the north shore of Kaua'i. JAMES RANDKLEV

Butterflyfish and slate-pencil urchins are among the wonders this snorkeler has discovered while exploring a coral reef.   JAMES D. WATT / INNERSPACE VISIONS

Fine white sand, crystal-clear water, and a lack of strong currents make the beach at Kapalua Bay one of the best and safest on Maui. ANN CECIL

A blackside hawkfish hovers motionless amid the branches of a coral head, waiting for prey. JAMES D. WATT / INNERSPACE VISIONS

66 *A foray [to the coral reef] is like a visit to a neighboring planet: a mystery, a magic formation of tiny animals sculpting fantastic shapes. The reef is alive with purple, green, orange, black, yellow, pink, blue, red, spotted, striped, stingered, spined, squirting, and tentacled creatures.* 99

Andrea Pro

At twilight, Waikiki dons exquisite evening attire of purple velvet trimmed with gold.   ANN CECIL

Most tourists cannot resist the islands' souvenir shops
and glitzy boutiques.   WANKE / WATAMURA / DEFINITIVE STOCK

17

Sunbathers soak up the rays in front of the Royal Hawaiian Hotel——the Pink Lady——
the traditional heart of Waikiki Beach.   JON GNASS / GNASS PHOTO IMAGES

*" It was tranced luxury to sit
in the perfumed air and forget
that there was any world but
these enchanted islands. "*

Mark Twain

A sun worshipper works on her tan and catches up on her reading
at Hoʻokipa Beach, Maui.   KERRICK JAMES

A couple of kayakers head for the calm waters off Lanikai Beach, O'ahu. GREG VAUGHN

The vivid hues and heavenly fragrance of Hawaiian leis help to make them the perfect symbol of "aloha."   ANN CECIL

> *The Hawaiian race is a kindly and affectionate one, hospitable and helpful one to the other; a race grateful to those who have been good to them. Such were the ways of the Hawaiians of old days.*
>
> Kepelino Keauokalani

A young hula dancer draped with plumeria leis prepares to perform with her *halau*, or dance troupe.   GREG VAUGHN

The bronze statue of King Kamehameha in Honolulu is traditionally wreathed in leis when islanders celebrate the great chief's birthday on June 11.   ANN CECIL

A lithesome Tahitian-style dancer exhibits her grace and skill. ANN CECIL

Tourists gamely try to learn the hula at a Hawaiian luau.   KERRICK JAMES

" In hula, more than technical perfection, you have to learn that love and passion come first. This has to be evident both spiritually and physically, for dance is the window to your soul. "

Maelia Loebenstein

> *Up, up, up rose the mountain wall, massive at its base where it knelt upon the earth, thin as the crest of a helmet where its head brushed against the clouds. Like a warrior it was, offering homage to his lord, and like feathers upon his helmet and cape were the trees, the shrubs, the ferns, and the grasses adorning its sides.*

O. A. Bushnell

These yellow-billed cardinals add to the vibrance of Hawai'i. ROBERT E. BARBER

Razor-sharp ridges and plunging ravines protect the enchanting Kalalau Valley on Kaua'i from all
but the most determined backpackers.   JAMES RANDKLEV

The Kalalau Trail leads to this golden stretch of sand, a "pot of gold" at the end of the rainbow.   TOM TILL

A carpet of emerald covers beach rock at Haʻena Beach on the north shore of Kauaʻi.   MARK W. LISK

Spectacular waterfalls slice thair way through the lush greenery of Kaua'i.   DAVID R. FRAZIER

The pale light of dawn heralds a new day at Lumaha'i Beach on the alluring north shore of Kaua'i.   STEVE MULLIGAN

The dying sun sets the sand ablaze at Molokaʻi's Papohaku Beach, one of the largest in the Hawaiian Islands.   TOM TILL

Guests enjoy a refreshing dip in the pool at the Hyatt Regency Hotel Resort at Lahaina, Maui. JAMES RANDKLEV

" You cannot take anything, including yourself, too seriously for very long in Hawaii.... [C]onditions in Hawaii are just too relaxing: the islands are lovely; the weather is superb; the music is gentle. Even the language is soothing: all the words sound like 'aaaahhhh.'"

Dave Barry

Swimmers staying at Ihilani, an O'ahu resort, must choose between the hotel pool and four ocean lagoons. PETER FRENCH

The Hilton Waikoloa Village in Kamuela offers its guests unique transport around the hotel's extensive grounds.   GREG VAUGHN

For the antique lover, the Manele Bay Hotel on Lana'i is lavishly decorated with exquisite objets d'art.   DAVE G. HOUSER

The Wai'oli Congregational Church occupies the grounds of one of the earliest Christian missions established in Hawai'i.   LARRY ULRICH

66 *Attaining Paradise in the hereafter does not concern me greatly. I was born in Paradise.* 99

Armine von Tempski

Lava rocks are the building blocks of Christ Memorial Episcopal Church in Kilauea.   JON GNASS / GNASS PHOTO IMAGES

The murals and frescos of St. Benedict's Painted Church, near Kona on the Big Island, were created by a Belgian priest in 1903. DAVID R. FRAZIER

Jogging barefoot into the sunset on O'ahu's north shore produces the ultimate "runner's high."   ANN CECIL

❝ Relax by the fireplace with a planter's punch and enjoy this special place. Look out across all of central Maui, to the ocean on each side, west to Lanai Island, and northwest to Molokai. All sunsets here are incomparable, no matter what the weather. ❞

Robert Wenkam

Sunset transforms Ala Moana Beach in Honolulu into a vibrant slice of South Seas paradise.   ANN CECIL

> *Oh, for this pulsing, undulating, shimmering, sighing, breathing plasma of an ocean. For the miracle of warm water. For rideable waves and no wind.*
>
> Thomas Farber

A statue of Duke Kahanamoku, "father of modern surfing," gazes over Waikiki Beach. CHEYENNE ROUSE

A lone boogie boarder challenges a monster wave at legendary Waimea Bay on O'ahu. ANN CECIL

The Surf and Sea Store in Hale'iwa on O'ahu is an example of an old, plantation-style building that was recycled to cater to tourists.   ANN CECIL

Popsicle-bright surfboards are the fashion for those wanting to catch a wave at Waikiki Beach.   ANN CECIL

Only the most experienced surfers dare challenge the tubular waves at the infamous Banzai Pipeline on O'ahu's north shore.   ANN CECIL

"Sand sharks" surround a gritty "surfer" as he waits for a big wave on the beach at Lahaina.
DOUG PERRINE / INNERSPACE VISIONS

*" There was more than
something in the idea that the
happiest Hawaiian was the native
paniolo.... The horse lifted him off
the ground, put him close to
nature, gave him a way to turn
his subtle perceptions and fleeting
impulses and superb reflexes into
sweeping motion. He had found
out how to surf the land. That was
happiness.* "

from *The Hawaiians*

A Hawaiian cowboy, or *paniolo*, rides herd at Kahua
Ranch in North Kohala, Hawai'i. GREG VAUGHN

40

The Parker Ranch, once the largest family-owned ranch in the nation, encompasses almost a quarter of a million acres.   PHILIP ROSENBERG

John Parker founded the Parker Ranch in 1847 with feral cattle and horses descended from stock presented as gifts to King Kamehameha I.   GREG VAUGHN

Paniolo at Kualoa Ranch reflect the ranching tradition of O'ahu as they gather to "talk story" and compete in rodeo-style events.   ANN CECIL

Calf roping is among the events attracting paniolo and spectators alike to the Kona Stampede, Honaunau, Big Island. GREG VAUGHN

This weatherworn paniolo no doubt has many a tale to tell of ranching in the early days. PETER FRENCH

Ancient petroglyphs, such as these near Olowalu, Maui, are found on all the main Hawaiian Islands, but in most cases their meaning and purpose remain a mystery. TOM TILL

❝ The shore is an ancient world, for as long as there has been an earth and sea there has been this place of the meeting of land and water. Yet it is a world that keeps alive the sense of continuing creation and of the relentless drive of life. ❞

Rachel Carson

A native islander crafts a nose flute, a musical instrument used by his ancestors. GREG VAUGHN

To prove their courage, the warriors of King Kamehameha dared to make this 60-foot plunge into the sea from Kahekili's Leap at Kaunolu, an ancient fishing village on Lana'i.   TOM TILL

Hawaiian women of the ruling class preferred to give birth at designated "birthing stones," like these in central O'ahu, believing that their labor would be eased and the birth propitious.   TOM TILL

> *There was the gaunt, hideous, desolate abyss, with its fiery cones, its rivers and surges of black lava and grey ash.... There never was a stranger contrast than between the hideous desolation of the crater below, and those blue and jewelled summits rising above the shifting clouds.*
>
> Isabella L. Bird, 1876

An offering to Pele, the tempestuous fire goddess, is left on the rim of Halemaʻumaʻu Crater.   ANN CECIL

Eruption and erosion have produced the 3,000-foot-deep crater atop Haleakala, a dormant volcano designated a national park in 1916. ANN CECIL

Dozens of tourists rise daily at 4 A.M. to watch the magnificent sunrise
from the top of Haleakala, the House of the Sun.   ANN CECIL

*❝ A growing warmth suffused the horizon, and soon the sun
emerged and looked out over the cloud-waste, flinging bars of ruddy
light across it, staining its folds and billow-caps with blushes.... It was
the sublimest spectacle I ever witnessed, and I think the memory of it
will remain with me always. ❞*

Mark Twain

The silversword, found only on desolate Haleakala, blooms only once in its 5- to 20-year existence and then dies.   LAURENCE PARENT

Thirty-five miles of hiking trails crisscross the floor of Haleakala Crater.   LARRY ULRICH

The eucalyptus tree, with its Technicolor trunk, was introduced to the islands
shortly after the turn of the 20th century.   TOM TILL

A swath of lacy fibers at the base of a coconut palm frond shrouds a morning glory vine.   LARRY ULRICH

A veil of water transforms lava rocks into glistening gems at Twin Falls on Highway 36, the Road to Hana.   STEVE MULLIGAN

A walk through this fern forest in Hawai'i Volcanoes National Park is a return to the island "forest primeval."   LARRY ULRICH

An iridescent anole searches the foliage for a tasty insect.   GREG VAUGHN

Ferns such as this *ama'uma'u* in Hawai'i Volcanoes National Park, are among the first plants to re-establish themselves on new lava flows.   GREG VAUGHN

66 *There was... no place known on earth that even began to compete with these islands in their capacity to encourage natural life to develop freely and radically up to its own best potential. More than nine out of ten things that grew here, grew no where else on earth.* **99**

James Michener

A fiddlehead from a native *uluhe* fern begins to unfurl toward the life-giving sun.   GREG VAUGHN

In the far reaches of Manoa Valley, only minutes from Honolulu, the Lyon Arboretum sits at the edge of the rain forest, the beginning of a different world.   TOM TILL

The endangered Hawaiian monk seal is one of only two mammals native to the islands. DAVID B. FLEETHAM / INNERSPACE VISIONS

> **❝** *In daydreams I have seen its face: a bulbous head covered in silvery fur, with black buttonhook-shaped eyes, a snout on which springy nostrils open full like quotation marks, tiny tab-shaped ears, a spray of cat's whiskers, and many doughy chins. On land, it drags itself with excruciating effort, or ripple-gallops like a four-hundred-pound slug. But the water sets it free to swivel and race.* **❞**

Diane Ackerman

A curious moray eel surveys its territory. KENNAN WARD

Rocky volcanic shores skirt the isolated beaches near South Point on the Big Island.   JAMES RANDKLEV

A sandbar shark casts a baleful eye at an intruder in his undersea domain.   DAVID B. FLEETHAM / INNERSPACE VISIONS

A green sea turtle gets a thorough cleaning as surgeonfish nibble algae from its shell.   DOUG PERRINE / INNERSPACE VISIONS

The early morning sun illuminates a silvery pathway to one of the Mokulua Islands along Kailua Beach on the windward side of O'ahu.   GREG VAUGHN

Octopus, red squirrelfish, and lobster comprise this young man's catch of the day.   DAVID R. FRAZIER

Deep-sea sport fishing is big business in Kailua-Kona, where thousands of dollars are at stake during an annual billfish tournament. PETER FRENCH

A short-nosed spearfish is hauled aboard from the blue waters off the Kona Coast. GREG VAUGHN

There is, one knows not what sweet mystery about this sea, whose gently awful stirrings seem to speak of some hidden soul beneath.

Herman Melville

Space-aged condominiums stab the skyline of Honolulu, the economic and business hub of the Pacific.   JAMES RANDKLEV

Spacious and modern, the new Honolulu Convention Center caters to large organizations and groups.   PETER FRENCH

❝ [Honolulu] is the meeting place of East and West. The very new rubs shoulders with the immeasurably old. And if you have not found the romance you expected you have come upon something singularly intriguing. ❞

W. Somerset Maugham

Boogie boarders head for the waves at Waiʻoli Beach, near Hanalei, Kauaʻi.   NANCY HOYT BELCHER

On hot, sunny days, nothing is more refreshing than "shave ice," a colorful
and delicious Hawaiian specialty.   ANN CECIL

Passing knowledge and lore from *kupuna* to *keiki*, or elder to child, is a centuries old Hawaiian tradition. ANN CECIL

This child's sparkling smile outshines even the brilliance of her colorful balloons. ANN CECIL

❝ Men and women looked as easy, contented, and happy as if care never came near them. I never saw such healthy, bright complexions as among the women, or such 'sparkling smiles,' or such a diffusion of feminine grace and graciousness anywhere. ❞

Isabella Bird

The *muu'muu*, the traditional dress of Hawaiian women, is highly popular with tourists as well. GREG VAUGHN

66 *Honolulu… boasts a fascinating blend of a multi-ethnic population and a lifestyle in which individuality reigns supreme—where muumuus and cutoffs, oxfords and bare feet, tuxedos and swimsuits intermingle in the restaurants and night clubs.… Long before first-time visitors to Hawaii flew over Diamond Head and Honolulu in a 747, they had been primed for pleasure. And for most people, there are no disappointments.…*

Robert Smith

A visitor tries her hand at making a lei at the Kona Village Resort on the Big Island. PETER FRENCH

A mecca for souvenir hunters, the International Market Place in Waikiki is crowded with stands offering trinkets and treasures.   PETER FRENCH

Korean tourists fill the boat for a tour of the Polynesian Cultural Center on O'ahu.   BUDDY MAYS / TRAVEL STOCK

> *" Bore off and made all sail for the Coast of China, and soon lost sight of these beautiful isles, The Inhabitants of which appear'd to me to be the happiest people in the world. Indeed there was something in them so frank and chearfull that you cou'd not help feeling preposses'd in their favour.... "*

John Boit, 1792

Big Island Cub Scouts visit Pu'uhonua o Honaunau National Historical Park. GREG VAUGHN

Fierce *ki'i* guard sacred *he'iau* grounds at Pu'uhonua o Honaunau National Historical Park, where a Keawe chief is buried. JAMES RANDKLEV

Byodo-In Temple, a replica of a 900-year-old Buddhist shrine in Japan, sits serenely at the base of the Koʻolau cliffs in Kaneʻohe, Oʻahu.   GREG VAUGHN

This imposing Buddha, dedicated to the first Japanese immigrants to Hawaiʻi, presides over the Lahaina Jodo Mission on Maui.   GREG VAUGHN

The Bishop Museum in Honolulu houses a treasure trove of Hawaiian and Polynesian artifacts; its insect collection alone contains 13.5 million specimens. PETER FRENCH

This fearsome representation of the war god Kuka'ilimoku is on display at the Bishop Museum. MICHAEL SAMPLE

" Living on isolated islands, we cherish our diversities. For we have come from many places and in many different ways to this enormous yet intimate chamber of summer. "

from *The Hawaiians*

The awesome pyrotechnic displays of Kilauea, the smallest but most active Big Island volcano, attract thousands of spectators each year. ANN CECIL

“ We gazed down upon a place
of fire and earthquake. The tie-
ribs of earth lay bare before us. It
was a workshop of nature still
cluttered with the raw beginnings
of world-making. ”

Jack London

Lava flows into the sea and adds to the landmass
of the Big Island.   MICHAEL SAMPLE

A curtain of fire heralds an eruption in the east rift zone of Kilauea Volcano, one of only two active volcanoes in Hawai'i.   GREG VAUGHN

" This was the restless surge of the universe, the violence of birth, the cold tearing away of death; and yet how promising was this interplay of forces as an island struggled to be born, vanishing in agony, then soaring aloft in triumph. "

James Michener

A break in the roof of a lava tube reveals a river of fire to the occupants of a hovering helicopter.   M. TIMOTHY O'KEEFE

At the Thurston Lava Tube in Hawai'i Volcanoes National Park, visitors can walk through a well-lit chamber that once was filled with molten lava.   PHILIP ROSENBERG

A fiery explosion occurs as red-hot lava collides with the cold sea.   PHILIP ROSENBERG

Pu'u O'o, a vent in the east rift zone of Kilauea, has covered thousands of acres of the Big Island with lava.   GREG VAUGHN

> **❝** *Kaua'i, though altogether different from Hawai'i, has an extreme beauty altogether its own, which wins one's love.* **❞**

Isabella L. Bird

After its harvest, the taro root is baked or pounded into the delicacy called *poi*. ANN CECIL

Taro fields in the beautiful Hanalei Valley, Kaua'i, do double duty, serving also as a sea bird refuge.   DAVID R. FRAZIER

Pineapple fields and plush resorts co-exist on Maui's west shore. The island of Lana'i appears in the distance.   ANN CECIL

Once a major crop on four of the Hawaiian Islands, pineapple is now grown only on O'ahu and Maui.   ANN CECIL

Just the right blend of weather, soil, and moisture allows the Kona highlands to produce one of the world's premier coffees. PETER FRENCH

In contrast to harvesting methods employed on the other islands, most Kona coffee is still picked by hand. GREG VAUGHN

Once grown only on Kona, coffee is now produced on all the main Hawaiian Islands. ANN CECIL

Funky stands along rural roads offer fresh fruits and vegetables to passing motorists.   ANN CECIL

The breadfruit, a staple food of Polynesia, grows in many Hawaiian back yards.   ANN CECIL

Bananas are a major crop in Hawai'i and are also found in many local gardens.   CHEYENNE ROUSE

Freshly picked papayas are ready to go to market.   DAVID R. FRAZIER

" Everything grew freely and with an energy that was, I thought, startling. It was as if the plants wanted to take over and hide anything human that might have been."

Marjorie Sinclair

Naupaka, a hardy beach native, thrives in the salt spray on the rocky coast north of Hana, Maui.   LARRY ULRICH

Small, rocky, and windswept, Alau Island, near Hana, wears a mantle of green and a crown of palms.   LARRY ULRICH

Highway 36, the Road to Hana, slithers through more than 600 curves as it follows the coastline to Maui's most popular small town. JAMES RANDKLEV

<blockquote>
" Islands are clothed by the sea.
Around the Hawaiian archipelago,
in sunny, trade-wind weather, they
flaunt their finery. "
</blockquote>

John L. Culliney

Roadside flower stands tempt drivers on
the Road to Hana. NANCY HOYT BELCHER

Wailua is one of many romantic waterfalls along the 52-mile Road to Hana. GREG VAUGHN

A roadside entrepreneur weaves palm fronds into hats to sell to motorists on the Hana Highway. LAURENCE PARENT

Pua'a Ka'a State Wayside, just off the Hana Highway, feels much more remote than it is.   LARRY ULRICH

> " *It is pleasant, above all, to wander by the margin of the sea.... Along the brink, rock architecture and sea music please the senses, and in that tainted place the thought of the cleanness of the antiseptic ocean is welcome to the mind.* "

Robert Louis Stevenson

A lei that washes back to shore is traditionally a sign that its owner will return to the island. JAMES RANDKLEV

A kayaker paddles through aquamarine waters toward the Mokulua Islands in Kailua Bay, O'ahu.   GREG VAUGHN

Young paddlers in an outrigger canoe venture up the Kahana River on the windward side of O'ahu.   GREG VAUGHN

66 *Strip off your clothes that are a nuisance in this mellow climate. Get in and wrestle with the sea; wing your heels with the skill and power that reside in you; bite the sea's breakers, master them, and ride upon their backs as a king should.* 99

Jack London

Jumping Rock, at Waimea Bay, O'ahu, is a magnet for those with derring-do.   ED WATAMURA / DEFINITIVE STOCK

A windsurfer takes to the air at Ho'okipa Beach Park, Maui, one of the world's premier sailboarding locations.   JAMES RANDKLEV

Paddling, especially in outrigger canoes, is a popular competitive sport. Close to 4,500 members are enrolled in the islands' 29 paddling clubs.   ANN CECIL

With ports of call on Kaua'i, Maui, and Hawai'i, cruise ships are one of the most popular ways to see the islands.   PETER FRENCH

Except for oil, most sea cargo bound for Hawai'i arrives on container ships like this one.   ANN CECIL

Puowaina, the "Hill of Human Sacrifice" now known as the Punchbowl, was aptly chosen as the site of the National Memorial Cemetery of the Pacific.   ANN CECIL

Today the USS Arizona *stands as a reminder of the events of that Sunday morning. It has different meanings for the millions who visit here. But to all of them it speaks silently but eloquently of the distance yet to be travelled before the world lives in peace.*

Michael Slackman

The USS *Arizona* Memorial rests above the remains of the sunken battleship and its entombed crew, victims of Pearl Harbor.   ANN CECIL

According to legend, this rocky stream in 'Iao Valley once ran red with the blood of Maui warriors defending their island from Kamehameha. CLINT FARLINGER

66 The places where these birds dwell are the quiet places of Hawai'i where few people venture. Birding in these uncrowded spots is a little like stepping back into the forests of long ago, to a time when a natural harmony embraced the land and newcomers had just begun to fashion these Islands into their own vision of paradise. 99

Rick Soehren

The nene, Hawai'i's state bird, is making a comeback after facing extinction at the dawn of the 20th century. GARY KRAMER

Norfolk Island pines, seen here in a grove at Waʻahila Ridge on Oʻahu, were prized for their tall, straight trunks and used to make masts for sailing ships.   MICHAEL SAMPLE

The red-crested cardinal is one of more than 150 species of birds introduced to the islands since 1796.   GARY KRAMER

A sunset stroll along a sandy beach ends a perfect day at Hale‘iwa Beach on O‘ahu's north shore.   JAMES RANDKLEV

The amaryllis now grows wild on the islands after escaping from domestic gardens. BUDDY MAYS / TRAVEL STOCK

This exotic flower with its multicolored "plumage" is aptly named "bird of paradise." BUDDY MAYS / TRAVEL STOCK

Adorned in pearls of dew, a morning glory greets the dawn. MICHAEL SAMPLE

The showy hibiscus is the official state flower and a trademark of the islands. GREG VAUGHN

" The wild places of Hawaii are extremely valuable, a handful of jewels on the green velvet sea, and what they contain is to the mainlander wondrously strange.... These things are not only rare but delicate—otherworldly and fragile as dreams. They are the plants and birds one imagines in the background of Shakespeare's Tempest. *Touch them and they vanish. "*

Robert Wallace

Dramatic cliffs tower over Oʻahu's Koʻolau Golf Course, reputedly the most difficult course in the nation.   ANN CECIL

66 *The marvelous temperature, which is never hot and never cold;... the rich and variable color; the fragrance so intense after a shower;... the irreproachable languor of a race that is the incarnation of these elements—this is quite as much as a man wants... and all this he has without the asking.* 99

Charles Warren Stoddard, 1892

Luxuriant courses like this one on Kapalua Bay make Maui one of the most attractive island golf destinations.   ANN CECIL

Sand and sea traps intimidate duffers at the 36-hole Francis I'i Brown Course on the Big Island.   JAN BUTCHOFSKY–HOUSER

Dawn breaks over the championship course at Princeville Resort on Kaua'i.   ANN CECIL

Sightseers must ascend the Wailua River in Kaua'i by boat to visit the Fern Grotto, a popular setting for Hawaiian weddings. GREG VAUGHN

A hiker walks through the mist high above Waipi'o, the largest and one of the most scenic valleys on the Big Island.   LAURENCE PARENT

The Kohala Ditch, built in 1906 to irrigate cane fields, now serves as a route for backpackers.   PHILIP ROSENBERG

      A sea of vegetation laved the landscape, pouring its green billows from wall to wall, dripping from the cliff lips in great vine masses, and flinging sprays of ferns and air plants into the multitudinous crevices.

Jack London

No luau is complete without a *kalua* pig baked in an *imu*, a pit in the earth lined with hot rocks.   GREG VAUGHN

66 *They eat and eat and eat.... beat their stomachs with satisfaction, they talk and eat, they ride about and eat again.... they laugh, sing and eat.... at last a man declares he can hold no more, he is* pau, *and he declares himself* mauna, *a mountain.* 99

Charles Nordhoff, 1874

A slice of cold watermelon is the perfect thirst-quencher after a day at the beach.   PHILIP ROSENBERG

Luau guests are awed by the show-stopping performance of the fire dance.   CHRISTIAN HEEB / GNASS PHOTO IMAGES

66 The playful Goddess was toying with the liquid fire, tossing up great handfuls and scattering it about in showers of fiery spray. Small patches of evanescent flame would dart upward and burn brilliantly for a few moments, and then slowly dying out, would be succeeded by others equally beautiful, brought forth like their predecessors to live the same short but 'shining' life. 99

George Stewart, 1881

Hanauma Bay is the most popular snorkeling destination in the islands, and its fish have been known to nip if not offered a tidbit or two.   JAMES RANDKLEV

❝ ...that peaceful land, that far-off home of profound repose, and soft indolence, and dreamy solitude, where life is one long slumberless Sabbath, the climate one long delicious summer day.... ❞

Mark Twain

While many challenge the surf at Sunset Beach, others prefer a more leisurely stroll in the sun.   MAXINE CASS

A frolic in the shorebreak is one of the joys of a day at the beach.   MICHAEL SAMPLE

A tunnel through the Maui Ocean Center aquarium in Maʻalaea allows visitors a fish-eye view of some of Hawaiʻi's colorful sea creatures. ANN CECIL

Three *Atlantis* submarines, in Waikiki, Lahaina, and Kona, allow tourists to enjoy underwater scenery without getting wet.   DAVID R. FRAZIER

Both parties seem to enjoy an encounter in the manmade lagoon of the Hilton Waikoloa Village, Big Island.   M. TIMOTHY O'KEEFE

A tour boat plies the 12-mile-long Wailua River, the only navigable waterway in the islands.   JAMES RANDKLEV

Behind us ropy waterfalls cascade thousands of feet to overflow the deep, dark valley pools, to wander and feed the fertile earth and, shimmering over pebbled shallows, to make music on their fretted journey to the sea.

from *The Hawaiians*

Unlike other water birds that only winter in the islands, the snowy cattle egret has become a year-round resident.   LEE FOSTER

On the southern boundary of Haleakala National Park, the many Pools of Ohe'o form a series of terraces on their way to the sea.   DAVE G. HOUSER

A fisherman casts into the sea at Keʻe Beach in Haʻena State Park, Kauaʻi.   ANN CECIL

A modern-day Robinson Crusoe leaves evidence of his passing on lonely Kuaehu Point, Kauaʻi.   MARK W. LISK

The setting sun kisses the dramatic contours of the Na Pali Coast in Kaua'i.   NANCY HOYT BELCHER

" On all these shores there are echoes of past and future: of the flow of time, obliterating yet containing all that has gone before; of the sea's eternal rhythms—the tides, the beat of the surf, the pressing rivers of the currents—shaping, changing, dominating; of the stream of life, flowing as inexorably as any ocean current, from past to unknown future. "

Rachel Carson

Volcanic remnants worn smooth by the sea litter the sand near Hoʻokipa Beach State Park, Maui.   JAMES RANDKLEV

Most black sand beaches, such as this one at Pailoa Bay, Maui, are composed of tiny crystals of volcanic glass.   LARRY ULRICH

The black-footed albatross breeds on the northwestern Hawaiian Islands
and elsewhere in the mid-Pacific.   KENNAN WARD

Once lush with sugar cane, fields on the Big Island's Hamakua Coast now lie fallow as sugar production wanes in Hawai'i.   LAURENCE PARENT

This native hala grove on the cliffs above Pailoa Bay at Wai'anapanapa State Park is one of the largest remaining stands in the islands.   LARRY ULRICH

Much of the pristine Kipahulu Valley, on the southern foot of Haleakala, is a restricted scientific research reserve.   LARRY ULRICH

Lahaina's Front Street blazes with light from stores and restaurants, some of which offer live entertainment. ANN CECIL

Railroads that once hauled passengers to town and sugar cane to market
now are used to shuttle tourists. ANN CECIL

The largest banyan tree in the nation sprawls above the courthouse square in Lahaina. STEVE MULLIGAN

they made it possible

Hawai'i on My Mind would have been impossible to produce without the keen eyes and technical skills of more than thirty professional photographers. These women and men submitted their finest images, and the results show in this stunning collection of photos. What does not show is the work it took to get these images— the early mornings to capture the sunrise, the long hikes through lava fields and rain forest, the endless hours of waiting for the perfect light, the hundreds of shots that didn't turn out quite right, and the high level of technical skill that was acquired through years of experience and study. To all the photographers who contributed to *Hawai'i on My Mind,* we say thanks. We appreciate their art and their hard work.

The Publishers

Photographers in *Hawai'i on My Mind*

Robert E. Barber
Nancy Hoyt Belcher
Jan Butchofsky-Houser
Ann Cecil
Maxine Cass
Clint Farlinger
Lee Foster
David R. Frazier
Peter French
Dave G. Houser
Kerrick James
Michelle Janica
Gary Kramer
Mark W. Lisk
Buddy Mays
Steve Mulligan
M. Timothy O'Keefe
Laurence Parent
James Randklev
Philip Rosenberg
Cheyenne Rouse
Michael Sample
Tom Till
Larry Ulrich
Greg Vaughn
Kennan Ward

Definitive Stock
   Ed Watamura

Gnass Photo Images
   Jon Gnass
   Christian Heeb
   Bruce Jackson

Innerspace Visions
   Phillip Colla
   David B. Fleetham
   Doug Perrine
   James D. Watt

Larry Ulrich Stock
   William Neill

ISBN 1-56044-823-7

Manufactured in Korea
First Edition/Second Printing

The Globe Pequot Press

www.globe-pequot.com

Front cover photo:
Hanalei Bay ANN CECIL
Front cover inset photo: Pineapple ANN CECIL
Back cover photos:
  Kalalau Valley, Kaua'i JAMES RANDKLEV
  Hawaiian monk seal DAVID B. FLEETHAM / INNERSPACE VISIONS
  Islander in one-man outrigger canoe ANN CECIL
  Lava collides with the Pacific Ocean PHILIP ROSENBERG
  Heliconia rostiata BUDDY MAYS / TRAVEL STOCK
End papers: Colorful Hawaiian leis GREG VAUGHN

acknowledgments

The publisher gratefully acknowledges the following sources:

Title page quote as reprinted in *And the View from the Shore: Literary Traditions of Hawai'i*, by Stephen H. Sumida. Seattle: University of Washington Press, 1991.

Pages 2 and 24 quotes from *Ka'a'awa: A Novel about Hawaii in the 1850s*, by O. A. Bushnell. Honolulu: The University Press of Hawaii, 1972.

Page 6 quote from *Mark Twain's Letters from Hawaii*, ed. by A. Grove Day. Honolulu: University of Hawaii Press, 1966.

Page 8 quote from "The Islands of Life," by Gavan Daws, in *A World Between Waves*, ed. by Frank Stewart. Washington, DC, and Covelo, CA: Island Press, 1992.

Page 11 quote from *Shark Dialogues*, by Kiana Davenport. New York: Atheneum, 1994.

Page 15 quote from "Teachings from the Reef," by Andrea Pro. *Ka'u Landing: A Magazine from the Island of Hawai'i*, August 1998.

Page 17 quote from *Whale Song: A Pictorial History of Whaling and Hawai'i*, by MacKinnon Simpson. Honolulu: Beyond Words Publishing, 1986.

Pages 18 and 48 quotes from *Roughing It*, by Mark Twain. New York: Harper & Bros., 1899.

Page 20 quote as reprinted in *The Spell of Hawaii*, ed. by A. Grove Day and Carl Stroven. New York: Meredith Press, 1968.

Page 23 quote from "Hula: The Loebenstein Legacy," by Debra Toy Bressem. *Honolulu*, April 1998.

Page 30 quote from "Dave Barry Does Hawaii," by Dave Barry. *Hana Hou! The Magazine of Hawaiian Airlines*, Summer 1998.

Page 32 quote from *Born in Paradise*, by Armine von Tempski. New York: Duell, Sloan and Pearce, 1940.

Page 34 quote from *Country Roads of Hawaii*, by Robert Wenkam. Castine, ME: Country Roads Press, 1993.

Page 36 quote from *On Water*, by Thomas Farber. Hopewell, NJ: Ecco Press, 1994.

Pages 40, 71, and 108 quotes from *The Hawaiians*, by Gavan Daws and Ed Sheehan. Norfolk Island, Australia: Island Heritage, 1970.

Pages 44 and 111 quotes from *The Edge of the Sea*, by Rachel Carson. Boston: Houghton Mifflin, 1955.

Pages 46, 65, and 76 quotes from *Six Months in the Sandwich Islands*, by Isabella L. Bird. Honolulu: University of Hawaii Press, 1964. Originally published by John Murray, London, 1876.

Pages 54 and 74 quotes from *Hawaii*, by James Michener. New York: Random House, 1959.

Page 57 quote from *The Rarest of the Rare*, by Diane Ackerman. New York: Random House, 1995.

Page 61 quote from *Moby Dick*, by Herman Melville. New York: Penguin Classics, 1992. Originally published in London, 1851.

Page 63 quote from *Trembling of a Leaf*, by W. Somerset Maugham. New York: Doubleday & Co., 1921.

Page 66 quote from "Hiking Above Waikiki," by Robert Smith. *Hawaii Magazine*, May/June 1998.

Page 68 quote as reprinted in *Images of Hawaii*, by Leonard Lueras. Hong Kong: Hong Kong Publishing Co., 1984.

Page 73 quote from "The House of the Sun," by Jack London, in *The Spell of Hawaii*, ed. by A. Grove Day and Carl Stroven. New York: Meredith Press, 1968.

Page 81 quote from "The Feather Lei," by Marjorie Sinclair, in *A Hawai'i Anthology*, ed. by Joseph Stanton. Honolulu: State Foundation on Culture and the Arts, 1997.

Page 85 quote from "Hawaii at the Edge," by John L. Culliney, in *A World Between Waves*, ed. by Frank Stewart. Washington, DC, and Covelo, CA: Island Press, 1992.

Page 88 quote from *Travels in Hawaii*, by Robert Louis Stevenson. Honolulu: The University Press of Hawaii, 1973.

Page 90 quote from *Learning Hawaiian Surfing*, by Jack London. Honolulu: Boom Enterprises, 1983. Originally published by The Crowell Publishing Co., 1907.

Page 93 quote from *Remembering Pearl Harbor: The Story of the USS* Arizona *Memorial*, by Michael Slackman, National Park Service. Honolulu: Arizona Memorial Museum Association, 1987.

Page 94 quote from *The Birdwatcher's Guide to Hawai'i*, by Rick Soehren. Honolulu: University of Hawai'i Press, 1996.

Page 97 quote from *Hawaii*, by Robert Wallace. New York: Time-Life Books, 1973.

Page 98 quote from *A Trip to Hawaii*, by Charles Warren Stoddard. San Francisco: Passenger Department, Oceanic Steamship Co., 1892.

Page 101 quote from *The House of Pride*, by Jack London. New York: Macmillan Co., 1912.

Page 102 quote from *Northern California, Oregon and the Sandwich Islands*, by Charles Nordhoff. New York: Harper & Bros., 1874.

Page 103 quote from *On the Rim of Kilauea: Excerpts from the Volcano House Register, 1865-1955*, ed. by Darcy Bevens. Hawaii National Park: Hawaii Natural History Association, 1992.

Page 104 quote as reprinted in *The Sage of the Sandwich Islands*, by Edward B. Scott. Lake Tahoe: Sierra-Tahoe Publishing, 1968.

Page 120 quote from "My Hawaiian Aloha," by Jack London, in *More Tramps Abroad*, by Mark Twain et al. Hartford: American Publishing Company, 1897.

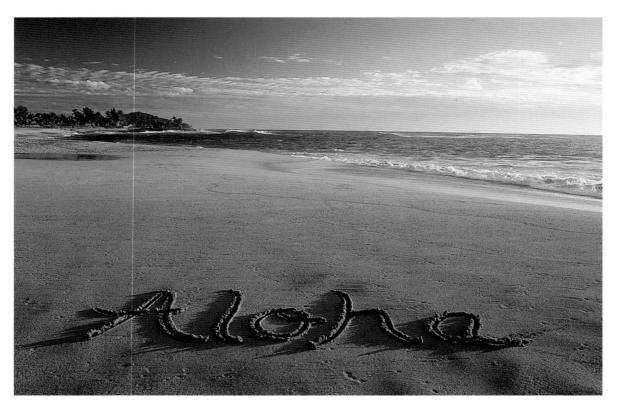

Aloha has many meanings, including both "farewell" and "welcome," so this greeting in the sand reminds a departing visitor that he will always be welcome in these lovely islands.   DAVID R. FRAZIER

❝ *In what other land save this one is the commonest form of greeting not 'Good day,' nor 'How d'ye do,' but 'Love?' That greeting is* Aloha— *love, I love you, my love to you…. It is a positive affirmation of the warmth of one's own heart-giving.* ❞

Jack London